Author
Maryann McMahon

The Author has been in the Academic Realm for 35 years as a Pre-Kindergarten, First, Fifth-and-Sixth Grade Teacher and is currently employed as an Educational Director.

Illustrator
Agata Olszewska

The Illustrator is a long-term Instructor of Early-Childhood and Elementary-School Children.

DEDICATION

"Vinnie and Vicki - The Vibrant Viruses!" is dedicated

TO MY MOM AND DAD,

who encouraged me to dream, to persevere and to reach for the stars.

But, most importantly, as authentic role models, they inspired me to make the world a better place for others!

A special thanks to Marijka Melnyk for all her technical help and support.

A portion of the proceeds will be generously donated to the education of poor and orphan children abroad, as well as local youngsters in need in the community.

VINNIE AND VICKI - THE VIBRANT VIRUSES!

Written by: Maryann McMahon

Illustrated by: Agata Olszewska

Vinnie and Vicki were two viruses who loved to get around.

They really enjoyed traveling all over town.

One very cold winter day, Vinnie and Vicki decided to visit a variety of places in their small village of Wheezeeview.

"WHERE SHALL WE GO FIRST?"

Vicki asked Vinnie excitedly.

They decided to visit the elementary school first. With great speed, the viruses flew through the air until they arrived at the big, red brick building. Then, they slipped silently underneath two heavy metal doors and carefully made their way down a long, wide hallway until they came to Mrs. Bookmark's first grade classroom.

The two viruses peeked in through a small glass window and viewed the classroom. They saw colorful pictures and posters scattered around the bright room. They could see a big sign in bold letters displaying the five vowels -- a, e, i, o, u.

Vinnie and Vicki made their move. They slowly slid through an opening under the classroom door. Mrs. Bookmark was busy reading a vivid tale of a volatile volcano in a land far, far away.

The two viruses began to eagerly roam around the cheerfully decorated classroom, veering left and right, to get a better view of some of the children's work which was hanging up on display.

They saw Vanessa's vocabulary quiz with the words:

bat, cat, hat, mat and sat; all spelled correctly.

They saw Victor's drawing of a kangaroo with a baby in its pouch.

Vicki and Vinnie remembered that kangaroos came from a faraway land called Australia.

Just then they heard, "ACHOO! ACHOO!"

"UH-OH!" Vinnie said. "IT'S HAPPENING AGAIN!"

The two viruses couldn't understand why everyone began to sneeze and cough whenever they entered a room. Soon, all of the boys and girls began to sneeze and cough -- even Mrs. Bookmark!

"I HOPE A VIRUS IS NOT GOING AROUND!" they heard Mrs. Bookmark say in a loud voice.

"HOW DOES SHE KNOW WE'RE HERE?" Vicki whispered to Vinnie.

The two viruses loved children very much and they hated to leave, but in their hearts, they knew it was time to go.

Vicki and Vinnie peered into other classrooms on the way out. They listened to Mr. Vicks teaching his fourth-grade class about George Washington's victory at Valley Forge.

"WASN'T GEORGE WASHINGTON THE FIRST PRESIDENT OF OUR COUNTRY?" Vicki questioned.

They passed by Mrs. Valley's second-grade class as she was writing a list of nouns and verbs on the Smartboard.

They smelled something delicious coming from Ms. Scrumptious'cooking class and heard Mr. Star discussing with his students how veterans are honored for their service to our country on Veteran's Day.

After leaving the school, the two viruses decided to visit the big shopping mall located in the middle of Wheezeeview.
There were a variety of stores in this vast place.

They swiftly passed by a toy store, a veterinary clinic, a library and a movie theater.

As Vinnie and Vicki were cheerfully zipping up and down the vertical escalator, they spotted an ice cream parlor on the second floor.

"LET'S GO IN!" said Vinnie excitedly.

The two viruses snuck in unnoticed and casually made their way to a booth where a lady and a little girl were busily licking vanilla ice cream cones. As they got closer, Vinnie and Vicki soon heard the familiar sounds of sneezing and coughing.

"YOU MUST BE GETTING A VIRUS,"
the woman said to her young daughter.

Vicki and Vinnie couldn't understand why everyone always became sick when they were around. That made them very sad indeed.

"WE'D BETTER LEAVE," Vinnie said.
"YES, IT'S TIME TO GO," Vicki agreed.
They certainly did not want to see anyone become ill.

They zoomed along rather unhappily.
"WHAT SHALL WE DO NOW?" asked Vicki.

The two viruses took a vote and decided to visit a nearby doctor's office. They had friends there - other viruses they had met in various places along the way. Vicki and Vinnie were anxious to see them again.

As they floated inside, they recognized Villi, Venus and Vector; three other viruses they knew. "WE'RE NOT WELCOME HERE," said Villi to the newcomers. "PEOPLE DON'T LIKE US. THEY ARE BLAMING US FOR MAKING THEM SICK!"

That's all Vinnie and Vicki heard people talking about -- viruses, viruses, viruses; and how to keep them away.

"I WONDER WHY PEOPLE BLAME US FOR THEIR TROUBLES?"

Vicki thought to herself.

Just then, a woman leaned over to her friend and said, "I CAN'T WAIT TO GET RID OF THIS VIRUS. I WISH WE COULD VACUUM UP ALL THE VIRUSES ON THIS EARTH AND SEND THEM TO THE MOON!"

Vicki and Vinnie didn't think that was very nice.

In the examining room, the two little viruses heard Dr. Vitality telling a young patient how to keep viruses away in order to stay healthy, strong and vigorous.

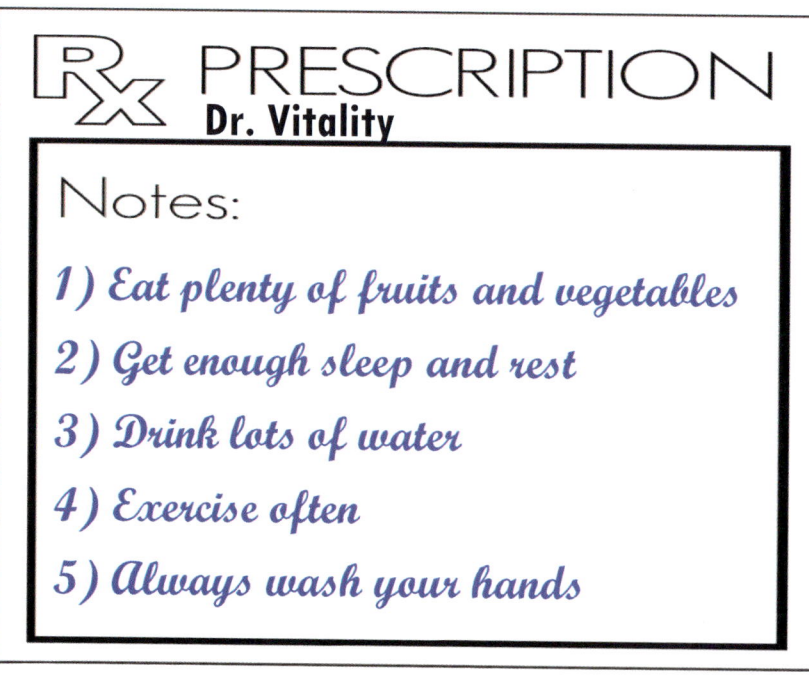

R̶x̶ PRESCRIPTION
Dr. Vitality

Notes:

1) Eat plenty of fruits and vegetables
2) Get enough sleep and rest
3) Drink lots of water
4) Exercise often
5) Always wash your hands

At this point, Vinnie and Vicki decided they had heard and seen enough. They knew they were not wanted here. So together with Villi, Venus and Vector, the two little unwanted viruses took a long voyage to a land far away, where there were no human beings -- because viruses and humans cannot live together in harmony.

And all the little viruses lived happily ever after!

VINNIE AND VICKI - THE VIBRANT VIRUSES!

WRITTEN BY: MARYANN MCMAHON

ILLUSTRATED BY: AGATA OLSZEWSKA

Made in the USA
Columbia, SC
29 August 2018

Made in the USA
Columbia, SC
29 August 2018